DATE DUE FOR RETURN

EASTERN STEAM
in camera

**John Adams and
Patrick Whitehouse**

LONDON
IAN ALLAN LTD

First published 1977

ISBN 0 7110 0805 1

Published by Ian Allan Ltd, Shepperton, Surrey, and
Printed in the United Kingdom by
Ian Allan Printing Ltd.

Above: A Gresley LNER Class K3 2-6-0 as BR No 61811
on a down freight approaching Potters Bar in
1950./*P. M. Alexander*

Above right: First of the class: BR Standard Class 7
Pacific No 70000 *Britannia* with the down 'Norfolkman'
in 1951./*P. M. Alexander*

Introduction

Steam in the east of Britain lasted well into 1967, though in the latter years it was restricted to the mineral trains in the Tyne Dock area of the old North Eastern Railway. Because of the old LNER's locomotive policy of keeping the best classes of its pre-grouping constituents in service, variety was one of the advantages the enthusiast enjoyed; indeed, some of the last steam engines to run were themselves from the North Eastern Railway — the P3 0-6-0s and the Q6 0-8-0s.

Over the period of Nationalisation many of the well-known classes went to the scrapheap, partly on account of steam modernisation and partly, of course, due to the coming of the diesel. Examples of the former were the advent of the 'Britannias', which revolutionised the East Anglian workings, displacing the 'Sandringhams' and the Great Eastern 4-4-0s, whilst branch line dieselisation saw the end of the Class E4 2-4-0s; final dieselisation, the Beeching axe and its aftermath did the rest.

The 1950s, however, were full of spice. The close of 1950 itself saw one of the first of many 'last runs' — that of the Great Northern Class C1 Atlantic No 62822 — whilst less than two years later Alan Pegler and his friends brought out the two preserved GN 4-4-2s and ran them on the 'Plant Centenarian'. Pegler was to prove a name in the land with his purchase of No 4472 *Flying Scotsman*, the first main-line express engine to be preserved and run in private hands. Then there were the exploits of Bill Hoole with the now preserved

Above: Ex-NER Class B16 4-6-0 No 61436 enters Selby with a tanker train in May 1953. Note the surviving NER slotted signals./*P. M. Alexander.*

Left: Crimple Junction near Harrogate in May, 1953, and an express headed by Class D49 4-4-0 No 62738 *The Zetland.*/*P. M. Alexander*

A4 Pacific No 4498 *Sir Nigel Gresley*, the introduction of the 'Elizabethan' express and the continuation of the luxury trains — for example the 'Tees-Tyne Pullman' and the 'Master Cutler'. As the sixties crept in, steam, like some ancient tribe hard pressed by the invader, was gradually driven north-eastwards and it was the freight workhorses of that era which fought the last battle — some to be kept for working tourist lines of the future.

Eastern Steam in Camera takes a look at the lines of the LNER south of the Scottish border, their trains and their engines. It is now ten years since regular steam ran over these tracks, though in many ways it seems but yesterday. This may well be due to the proliferation of LNER types extant on the tourist lines or that Parade of Parades, Shildon 1975. Whatever the truth of the matter these pages provide a nostalgic look at Eastern Steam, combining evocative scenes with a piece of railway history. Dates have been included in the captions where possible so that particular and peculiar engine workings can be noted for posterity. They were interesting and enjoyable times.

Gresley Class A3 Pacific No 60077 *The White Knight* passes Wortley Junction, Leeds, with a Liverpool to Newcastle express via Harrogate./*Eric Treacy*

Above: Potters Bar, 28 April 1951: Class B1 4-6-0 No 61138 heads a Kings Cross to Hitchin semi-fast./*P. M. Alexander*

Below: A Class K3 2-6-0 approaches Selby, Yorkshire. Note the ex-North Eastern Railway slotted signal gantry still in use./*P. M. Alexander*

Right: A down Newcastle express leaves York behind Class A4 Pacific No 60018 *Sparrow Hawk* of Gateshead Shed./*Eric Treacy*

60018
GATESHEAD
A-4

Above: Potters Bar, 28 April 1951, with Class V2 2-6-2 No 60879 on a down empty stock train./*P. M. Alexander*

Below: LNER Class N2/4 0-6-2T No 69576 on a down Kings Cross to Hatfield stopping train passing Potters Bar on 28 April 1951./*P. M. Alexander*

Above: Pegler's Special: the two Ivatt Great Northern Atlantics take the empty stock out of Doncaster after arriving from Kings Cross with the 'Plant Centenarian' on 20 September 1953./*P. B. Whitehouse*

Below: Hadley Wood, 26 November 1950: Class C1 4-4-2 No 62822, the last of the Ivatt Atlantics in service, on her final journey from Kings Cross to Doncaster, at the conclusion of which she was withdrawn for scrapping./*P. M. Alexander*

Above: Ex-GNR Class C12 4-4-2T No 67365 at Stamford on 26 May 1953./*P. M. Alexander*

Below: Ex-GNR Class C12 4-4-2T No 7374 on London's Palace Gates branch./*P. M. Alexander*

Above: Langley Water Troughs, 14 August 1949: Class B1 4-6-0 No 1258 takes water at the head of a Cambridge to Kings Cross express./*P. M. Alexander*

Below: Not yet repainted in British Railways' livery, in May 1948, is No 9000, Thompson's Class L1 2-6-4 tank prototype built for the LNER in 1945./*P. M. Alexander*

Left: Gresley Class K3 2-6-0 No 61879 heads a freight at Marshalls Meadows near Berwick./ *Eric Treacy*

Above: Littlebury, on the Liverpool Street-Cambridge main line, on 25 May 1951. Class K1 2-6-0 No 62031 on an up freight climbs the bank between Great Chesterford and Audley End./*P. M. Alexander*

Below: LNER Class P1 2-8-2 No 2393 at Peterborough New England shed in 1934. The class of two engines was withdrawn during the first years of Nationalisation./*A. W. Flowers*

Above: A down Newcastle express leaves York behind Class A2 Pacific No 60526 *Sugar Palm./Eric Treacy*

Top right: Gresley Class A4 Pacific No 60021 *Wild Swan* with an up vans special on Langley Troughs in August 1949./*P. M. Alexander*

Right: Langley Troughs, 8 August 1949: Class A4 4-6-2 No 60028 *Walter K. Whigham* (in dark blue livery) on an up express./*P. M. Alexander*

Left: Melton Constable, 23 May 1951: D16/3 4-4-0 No 62620 drawing the Cromer portion of a Yarmouth — Kings Lynn train forward to shunt across to the up platform./*P. M. Alexander*

Above: Near Ely, 24 May 1951: BR Standard 4-6-2 No 70007 *Coeur de Lion* crossing the Fens with a Liverpool Street to Norwich train via Cambridge./*P. M. Alexander*

Below: Class D16/3 4-4-0 No 62613 approaching Ketton & Collyweston, on the ex-MR Peterborough-Leicester line, with a Hunstanton to Leicester summer special on 4 July 1959. These through weekend workings used this route when the through M&GN line from Saxby Junction to Lynn was closed./*P. H. Wells*

Left: Framlingham, 21 May 1951: Ex-GER Class J15 0-6-0 No 65467 with the 6.8 p.m. Wickham Market to Framlingham branch train./*P. 'M. Alexander*

Above: Melton Constable, 23 May 1951: Class D15 4-4-0 No 62538 with the daily goods from Cromer. Note the M&GN somersault signals./*P. M. Alexander*

Below: Melton Constable, 23 May 1951: Class D16/3 4-4-0 No 62523 leaving with the Kings Lynn portion of a Yarmouth to Lynn train, with coaches for Cromer./*P. M. Alexander*

Above: Great Chesterford, 25 May 1951, with ex-WD
2-8-0 No 90294 on an up freight from
March./*P. M. Alexander*

Right: Chippenham Junction, near Newmarket, 25 May
1951: Class J17 0-6-0 No 65521 opens up as she rounds the
sharp curve to Chippenham Junction Box with a March
to Bury St Edmunds goods./*P. M. Alexander*

Near Kimbolton, Norfolk, 23 May 1951: Ex-GER No 1786 as Class D16 4-4-0 No 62617 with an East Dereham to Norwich train via Wymondham./*P. M. Alexander*

Above: Melton Constable Shed, 23 May 1951: left to right - Class D15 4-4-0 No 62528, Class D15 4-4-0 No 62538 and Class F4 2-4-2T No 67162./*P. M. Alexander*

Right: Kings Lynn, 24 May 1951: Class F6 2-4-2T No 67227 with the auto-train running between South Lynn and Kings Lynn./*P. M. Alexander*

Below: A Mildenhall branch train at Isleham, on 5 October, 1957 headed by Class J15 0-6-0 No 65438./*H. C. Casserley*

Above: Near Thetford, 25 May 1951: Class B17/1 4-6-0 No 61638 *Melton Hall* on a Liverpool Street to Norwich train./*P. M. Alexander*

Below: Santon Downham, Thetford, 15 May 1951: Thompson Class B1 4-6-0 No 61048 with a Liverpool Street to Norwich express./*P. M. Alexander*

Above: Thetford, 25 May 1951: Class F6 2-4-2T No 67237 approaching Thetford Bridge station on the Bury St Edmunds branch line with the 8.15 a.m. Thetford to Bury./*P. M. Alexander*

Below: Class J17 0-6-0 No 65528 on Coldham's Curve, Cambridge with the daily freight for the Mildenhall branch, on 8 March 1961. Note that: the locomotive is one of the few J17s with small tenders; the check rails, because of the severe curvature necessary when the route from Sixmile Bottom was realigned to make a junction with main line at Coldham's Lane Junction; the train is leaving for Mildenhall via the Newmarket line, but will return via Bottisham & Barnwell Junction; and the ex-GER skysign distant signal./*M. J. Fox*

Left: Audley End, 16 May 1951: ex-GER Class E4 2-4-0 No 2783 with the morning freight from Saffron Walden to Audley End. Note that this engine still carries its LNER livery and number./*P. M. Alexander*

Above: Cambridge University Railway Club Special at Mildenhall on 28 November 1959. The engine is the then sole remaining GER Class E4 2-4-0 No 62785./*G. D. King*

Below: Bury St Edmunds, 13 August 1949: Ex-GER Class J15 0-6-0 No 65451 takes the tablet from the signalman at the Junction box. The train is the 1.55 p.m. to Marks Tey./*P. M. Alexander*

Top left: Bury St Edmunds 13 August 1949. 'Super Claud' 4-4-0 No 62615 leaves with a down semi-fast./*P. M. Alexander*

Left: Near Kimberley Park, Norfolk, 23 May 1951. Class D16/3 4-4-0 No 62577 with the 10.26 Wymondham to East Dereham stopping train./*P. M. Alexander*

Above: One of Thompson's two-cylinder Class B2 4-6-0 rebuilds of the Gresley three-cylinder Class B17, No 61644 *Earlham Hall*, near Marks Tey with a down fast in 1949./*P. M. Alexander*

Above: Right up to the mid-1950s the ex-GER Class E4 2-4-0s were hard at work in East Anglia. Here is 'Intermediate' No 62781 on a Marks Tey train in May 1951./*P. M. Alexander*

Below: Thaxted, Suffolk, 26 May 1951: Ex-GER Class J67/2 0-6-0T No 68609 leaving for Elsenham with the 12.50 p.m. train./*P. M. Alexander*

Above: Kings Lynn, 24 May 1951: Class D16/3 4-4-0 No 62601 leaving with the 9.30 a.m. to Liverpool Street./*P. M. Alexander*

Below: Santon Downham, near Thetford, 24 May 1951: Class J39 0-6-0 No 64802 on an up cattle train./*P. M. Alexander*

Above: Little Glenham, near Wickham Market, 21 May 1951: Class D16/3 No 62611 on the daily Yarmouth to Ipswich milk train./*P. M. Alexander*

Top right: North Wootton, near Wolferton, 24 May 1951: Class D15 4-4-0 No 62506 with a Kings Lynn to Hunstanton train./*P. M. Alexander*

Right: Ex-GER 2-4-0 No E2794 approaching Marks Tey in May 1951. Note that the engine carries the early style BR numbering — that of the Region, E, in front of the old LNER number./*P. M. Alexander*

Above: Norwich (Thorpe) 22 May 1951: Class B17/1 4-6-0
No 61625 *Raby Castle* on a Liverpool Street to Norwich
train./*P. M. Alexander*

Top right: Whitlingham Junction, Thorpe-by-Norwich,
22 May 1951: Class D16 4-4-0 No 62555 with a Norwich to
Yarmouth train, skirting the banks of the River
Yare./*P. M. Alexander*

Right: Norwich (Thorpe), 22 May 1951: BR Standard
4-6-2 No 70007 *Coeur de Lion.*/*P. M. Alexander.*

Wymondham, 23 May 1951: BR Standard 4-6-2 No 70007
Coeur de Lion on a Norwich to Liverpool Street via
Cambridge./*P. M. Alexander*

Top left: Santon Downham, near Thetford, 25 May 1951: Gresley Class K3 2-6-0 No 61948 with a Peterborough to Norwich train./*P. M. Alexander*

Left: Near Dedham, 20 May 1951: a Gresley rebuild of Holden's GER Class B12 4-6-0 as B12/3 No 61570 on the 2.35 p.m. (Sundays) Norwich to Liverpool Street./*P. M. Alexander*

Above: Belstead, 21 May 1951: Thompson Class B1 4-6-0 No 61046 with the up 'East Anglian'./*P. M. Alexander*

Top left: Evening excursion: double-headed train for Darlington ready to leave Penrith behind two ex-NER Class J21 0-6-0s. Note that the leading engine is one of the Kirkby Stephen bankers with coupling hook detachment device on the front of the smokebox./*P. B. Whitehouse.*

Left: Belsted Cutting, near Ipswich, 21 May 1951: Standard BR Class 7MT Pacific No 70003 *John Bunyan* on the down 'Norfolkman'./*P. M. Alexander*

Above: Moulsworth Junction, Cheshire, with a CLC Chester to Manchester train behind ex-GCR Class D9 4-4-0 No 62304./*P. M. Alexander*

Above: Chester, Northgate, 29 May 1951: Class D10 4-4-0 'Director' No 62651 *Purdon Viccars* on the 6.45 p.m. train to Manchester Central./*P. M. Alexander*

Below: Knutsford, Cheshire, on 7 May 1949: Ex-GCR Class D9 4-4-0 No 62312 on a Manchester to Chester train passes 'ex-shops' Class J10 0-6-0 No 65128 on a Manchester to Knutsford special./*P. M. Alexander*

Above: August Bank Holiday excursion to Skegness at Belgrave Road, Leicester in 1961, with Class B1 4-6-0 No 61142. This is the old GNR terminus./*G. D. King*

Below: A Leicester (Belgrave Road) to Skegness Bank Holiday Excursion on 6 August 1962 at Forest Road crossing, Leicester, behind Class B1 4-6-0 No 61281. The tracks on the overbridge are the Midland main line and the signal box, Humberstone Road./*P. H. Wells*

Top left: Cheshire Lines, 7 May 1949. Class D9 4-4-0 No 62312 climbing up from Knutsford with a Chester Northgate to Manchester Central train./*P. M. Alexander*

Left: An ex-GCR 4-4-2 tank of Class C13 as BR No 67429 at Chester in 1951./*P. M. Alexander*

Above: An ex-Great Central Robinson 0-6-0 of LNER Class J10 climbs up bank from Mouldsworth Junction to Delamere on the Cheshire Lines Committee's tracks in 1950./*P. M. Alexander*

Top left: Knutsford, Cheshire Lines Committee, in May 1951: ex-GCR Class C13 4-4-2T No 67414./*P. M. Alexander*

Left: Chester Northgate Shed, 19 May 1951, showing Class C13 4-4-2Ts Nos 67400 and 67413, ex-GCR Nos 1055 and 178 respectively; (No 1055 was built by the Vulcan Foundry in 1903 and No 178 at Gorton)./*P. M. Alexander*

Above: Near Knutsford, Class J11 0-6-0 No 64453 with a Manchester Central to Northwich train near Knutsford in May 1951./*P. M. Alexander*

Above: Ex-GCR 'Director' class 4-4-0 No 62650 *Prince Henry*, still in LNER black livery and very dirty, on duty over the Cheshire Lines Committee's tracks in 1949./*P. M. Alexander*

Below: Replacing the ex-GNR Class C12 4-4-2 tanks as motive power for this branch, ex-GCR Class N5 0-6-2T No 69262 nears Stamford Town with the 7.30 a.m. for Essendine./*P. H. Wells*

Right: Potters Bar, 28 April 1951: Class V2 2-6-2 No 60911 starts on the up relief road with a heavy freight train./*P. M. Alexander*

Above: Class A3 4-6-2 No 60096 *Sceptre* with a down express between Crimple Junction and Harrogate./*P. M. Alexander*

Top right: Great Northern design: Gresley's Class O3 2-8-0 No 3467 at Doncaster. The BR number of this engine was 63485./*John Adams*

Centre Right: Introduced by Robinson for the Great Central in 1911, the O4 class of the LNER was well tried. No 63802 was an O4/8 built as late as 1944, using a B1 4-6-0 boiler./*P. M. Alexander*

Bottom right: The North Eastern Class Q5/1 0-8-0, a Worsdell piston-valve engine of 1903. The original Q5s had slide valves and dated from 1901./*John Adams*

Portrait of an A3: No 60054 *Prince of Wales*./*Colourviews Picture Library*

Above: Class K4 2-6-0 in Birmingham: a visit of Viscount Garnock's *The Great Marquess* to Tyseley shed, March 1967./*P. B. Whitehouse*

Below: One of Gresley's ubiquitous Class J39 0-6-0s as BR No 64943 double-heads a North Eastern Railway B16 class 4-6-0 on the approach to Harrogate in 1949./*P. M. Alexander*

Above: Peppercorn Class A1 Pacific No 60143 *Sir Walter Scott* with double chimney enters Selby station (north end) on an up express in May, 1953./*P. M. Alexander*

Below: An ex-LNER Class B16 4-6-0 as BR No 61472 at York in June 1955./*C. F. H. Oldham*

Left: An unidentified Class B16 4-6-0 takes a tanker train through Crimple Junction in May, 1953./*P. M. Alexander*

Right: LNER 'Hunt' class nameplate *The Craven.*/*P. M. Alexander*

Below: Crimple Junction near Harrogate, 28 May 1953: Class B16/1 4-6-0 No 61447 (ex-NER) rounds the sharp curve (speed limit 20 mph) from the Leeds line to join the Wetherby to Harrogate line through Prospect Tunnel./*P. M. Alexander*

Left: Class B16 4-6-0 No 61442 leaving Selby (Yorkshire) on an up express in May 1953./*P. M. Alexander*

Above: Knaresborough, Yorkshire, 28 May 1953: Class D49 4-4-0 No 62773 *The South Durham* climbs the 1 in 114 gradient to Starbeck with the 8.15 a.m. from Knaresborough to Harrogate and Leeds./*P. M. Alexander*

A fast freight headed by a Class V2 2-6-2 approaches
Gamston signalbox, near Retford, in September,
1957./*Eric Oldham*